SAFE RIDES

by Heidi Ward

TABLE OF CONTENTS

Model the Standard 2
TEXT 1 The Road to Car Safety 4
TEXT 2 Driving Into the Future of Car Safety 12
Glossary/Index 23
Answer Text Evidence Questions 24
Write to Sources .... Inside Back Cover

HOW TO READ THIS BOOK

1. Read the model lesson on pages 2–3.
2. Practice with the questions in the first text.
3. Apply the standard in the other text.
4. Answer the text evidence questions on page 24.

MODEL THE STANDARD

You will learn how to:

Explain Concepts and Procedures in a Text

A concept is a thought or idea. A procedure is a series of steps that describe or explain something. Readers can use specific information from the text to support their explanations of concepts and procedures. They can explain why a concept causes things to happen. They can explain what happens in a procedure and why each step is important.

To find specific information, ask: *What is important in this text? Why?* Then look for details that explain why the concept or procedure is important.

See how one reader answered questions by explaining why certain steps in a procedure are important.

Question 1: What concept is introduced in the second paragraph? How is it explained?

Answer: The text talks about wearing a helmet. It explains that wearing a helmet is the best way to protect yourself from injury.

Question 2: Why is it important to be visible when riding a bike?

Answer: Being visible is important because riders need to be seen by cars, pedestrians, and other bikers.

Bicycle Safety Procedures

Bike riding is fun, but you also need to follow the proper safety steps.

First, put on a bike helmet that fits you securely. In many states it is against the law to ride a bike without a helmet. Check the laws in your state. Regardless of the law, wearing a helmet is the best way to protect yourself from serious, or even fatal, injury.

> For Question 1, the reader identified the concept as well as details that explain the concept.

Next, check the equipment. Make sure the tires are inflated properly. Check that the brakes are working.

Maintain your balance. This is key to avoiding accidents. Adjust the bike to fit your height. Move your seat and handlebars to your height.

Be visible. You need to be seen by cars, pedestrians, and other bikers. Wear bright colors and reflective tape.

> For Question 2, the reader identified details that explain why it's necessary to be visible.

Finally, follow the rules of the road. Ride with the traffic. Obey all traffic signs and signals. Know and use hand signals to indicate you are stopping and turning.

> Turn the page to begin reading two texts about car safety. As you read, look for details that will help you explain important procedures.

TEXT 1

The Road to
CAR SAFETY

When Safety Is Extreme

It was a late evening in the summer of 2015. Stock car auto racing fans were at a race. Two hours into the main event, a car hit the one in front of it. That caused more cars to crash. Suddenly, there was chaos. Twenty-four cars were spinning and skidding out of control. Driver Austin Dillon's car hit another car. Dillon's car flipped over and flew into the fence surrounding the racetrack. Then it landed back on the track, spinning upside down. Emergency workers raced to the car. Amazingly, Dillon was unhurt. He waved to the worried crowd through the window.

▲ Auto racing has become a safer sport through the years. These devices protect the head and neck.

Austin Dillon spoke to reporters after his accident.

"[I] just wanted to wave to the fans and let them know I was all good.

I feel like it was the safety [features] that made it possible for me to be here today. I think it's pretty impressive to see how far we've come after learning from other wrecks."

Austin Dillon's car was made with important safety features. These features protected him from serious injury. First of all, his car's engine was pushed out during the crash so that it didn't hit him. Second, Dillon was harnessed into his seat, which was attached to a roll cage. A roll cage protects the driver in a rollover. Third, when Dillon hit the fence, an area of his car known as the crumple zone collapsed. This reduced the force of the impact. Lastly, Dillon wore a helmet, a **fire-retardant** suit, and something called a HANS (Head and Neck Support) device. This device protected his head and neck. These safety features helped Austin Dillon walk away from his crash.

What is one safety feature that protected Dillon? What details show that it was important?

THE ROAD TO CAR SAFETY

Years ago, cars did not have many safety features.

The Early Years of Car Safety

Safety has been a concern since people began driving cars. The first modern car was invented in the late 1800s. But it wasn't until the 1900s that cars became more common.

Early cars were open and could not protect passengers. They had hand brakes that worked well only if the car was moving slowly. As cars became faster and bigger, safety became more of a concern.

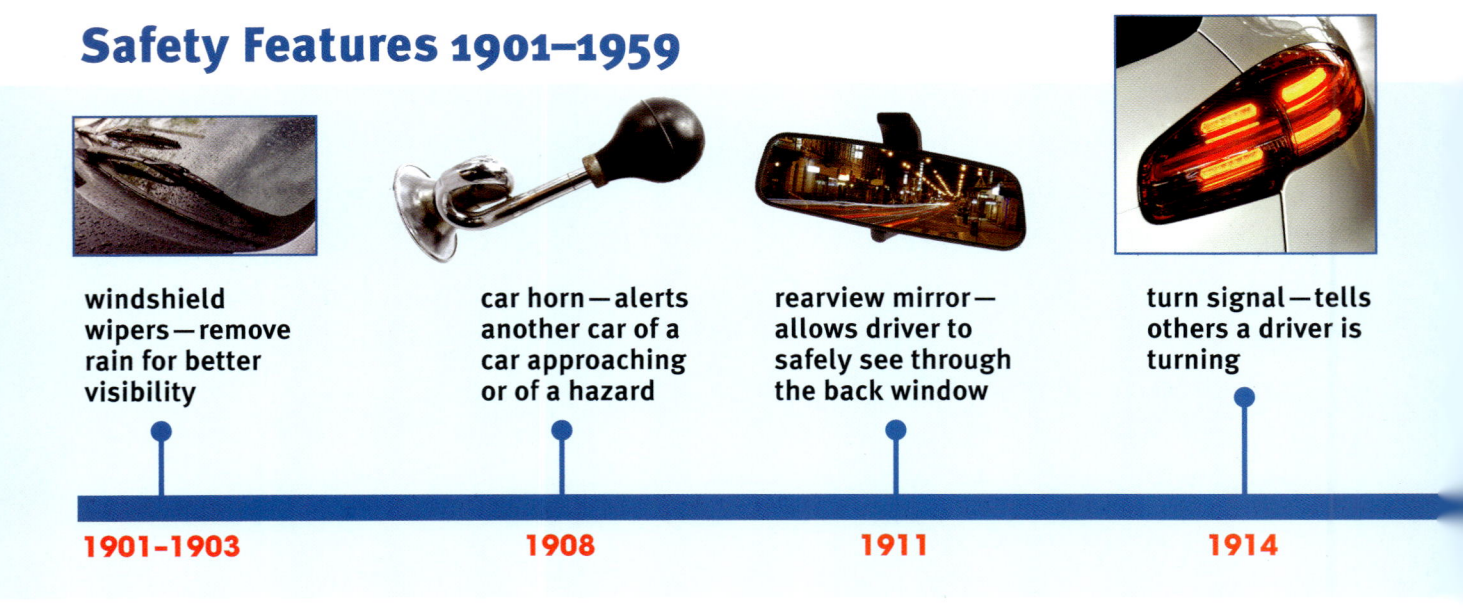

Safety Features 1901–1959

windshield wipers—remove rain for better visibility

car horn—alerts another car of a car approaching or of a hazard

rearview mirror—allows driver to safely see through the back window

turn signal—tells others a driver is turning

1901–1903　　**1908**　　**1911**　　**1914**

Throughout the first half of the twentieth century, important safety features were invented.

Early car brakes were made of wood that scraped against the tire when the driver pulled on them. In 1914, Fred Duesenberg created the first hydraulic brakes. These brakes used liquid-filled pipes to increase the pressure on the tire. This way, less force was needed to stop the car. Hydraulic brakes were more reliable than earlier brakes.

In 1903, a French scientist named Édouard Bénédictus developed safety glass. This glass did not shatter easily.

In the 1930s, a doctor named Claire Straith wrote about the need for safety features. He had seen many injuries from car accidents. He recommended that cars be made with padded dashboards.

In the 1940s, car manufacturer Preston Martin Tucker introduced both safety glass and padded dashboards, as well as lap seat belts. Eventually all cars would have padded dashboards and safety belts.

In 1958, the 3-point safety belt, or shoulder belt, was invented. This safer seat belt became the standard in all cars.

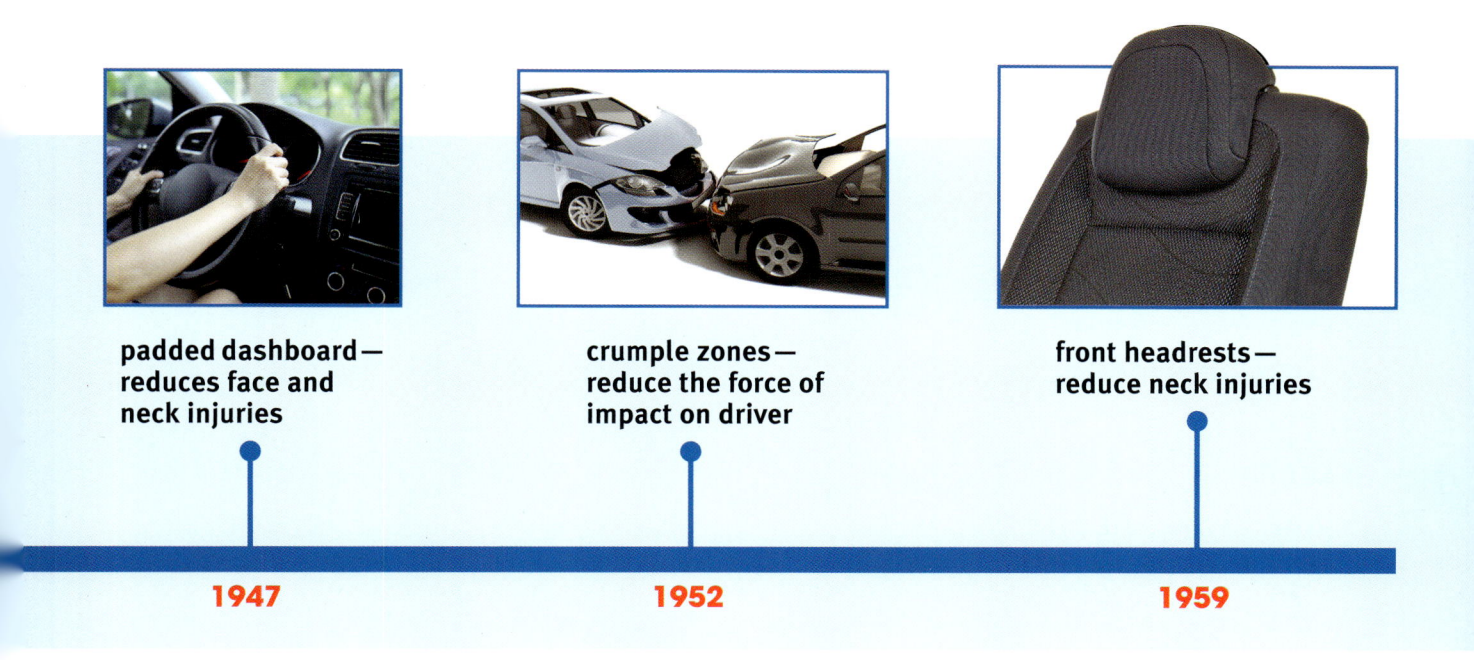

padded dashboard—reduces face and neck injuries

crumple zones—reduce the force of impact on driver

front headrests—reduce neck injuries

1947   **1952**   **1959**

THE ROAD TO CAR SAFETY

▲ Vince and Larry reminded drivers and passengers to stay safe.

Crash Test Dummies

Vince and Larry were plastic dummies that looked like people. They were created to show the effects of car **collisions** on people who did not wear seat belts.

Carmakers had always crashed cars to test their safety. But early crash tests did not have dummies in them. They could not accurately show how a crash affected a person. That changed in 1949 with Sierra Sam. He was a dummy created by the Air Force to test airplane safety. Automakers realized this was a good idea. They began using dummies in their crash tests.

Through the years, crash test dummies were created to test specific types of impact. Man-, woman-, and child-sized dummies were used.

Vince and Larry became the most famous crash test dummies. Their PSAs[1] from 1985 until 1998 inspired cartoons, a line of toys, and a video game. But more importantly, they helped people remember to wear their seat belts. Seat belt usage increased from 14 percent to 79 percent during this time. While Vince and Larry were not the only factor in that increase, they certainly made a memorable contribution.

1. PSA—A public service announcement is a message from the media to the public. It is made to raise awareness of an important issue.

Safety Features Working Together

A seat belt is designed to hold a person in place in a seat. According to the Centers for Disease Control and Prevention (CDC), seat belts reduce serious crash-related injuries and deaths by about half. Seat belt use is the most effective way to save lives and reduce injuries in car accidents.

An air bag inflates upon impact. A person hits the air bag instead of the hard parts of the car. Air bags save lives, but they do not reduce the importance of seat belts. Because air bags inflate extremely quickly, they can actually injure a person who is not wearing a seat belt.

Some people think that using either of these features alone provides enough protection. However, according to the CDC, air bags plus seat belts provide the best protection for drivers and passengers in a crash.

What happens after an air bag sensor detects a collision? Why is this important?

The 3-Point Safety Belt

Swedish engineer and inventor Nils Bohlin spent a year designing the 3-point safety seat belt. It has saved over a million lives. Bohlin wanted to create something simple enough to put on one-handed but that could protect the lower and upper body. Bohlin won numerous awards for this 1958 invention.

Air Bags

Air bags were first available in the 1970s. An air bag is folded into the steering wheel or dashboard. It acts like an inflating pillow that protects the driver. A sensor within the air bag tells it to inflate. When a car hits something, the inflation system fills the bag in less than a second. The bag has tiny holes in it, so another second later it is already deflating to get out of the driver's way.

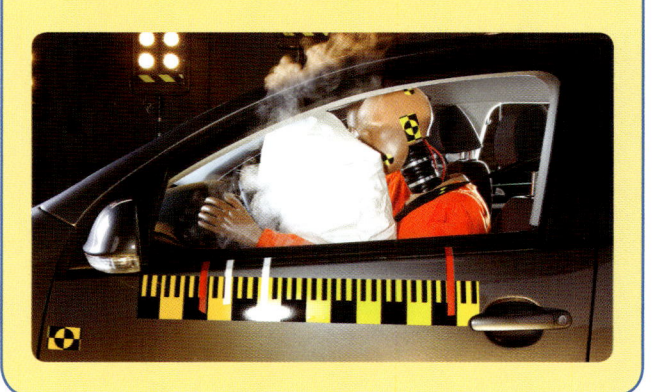

THE ROAD TO CAR SAFETY

▲ Booster seats are commonly used for older children. They help make sure the seat belt fits correctly.

Safety for All Passengers

Special consideration is given to the safety of babies and children in cars. Although child seats were around in the 1930s, their purpose was not safety. Early car seats were used so that children could see out the window and the driver could see them. It wasn't until the 1960s that car seat manufacturers began designing seats to protect children. But even then, the seats were used only to keep children from moving around in the car. Finally, in the mid-1970s, people began buckling their children in place in a car seat. Later, padding was added, as well as harness-style seat belts to hold babies or children still.

TEXT 1

Today, infant car seats are made to support a baby's delicate body. As a child grows, the correct type of car seat changes. The National Highway Traffic Safety Administration (NHTSA) is a government agency that sets car safety standards. NHTSA experts advise using a booster seat for all children who are shorter than 1.45 meters (4 ft 9 in) no matter how old they are or how much they weigh.

Why Don't School Buses Have Seat Belts?

The decision not to include seat belts on school buses was made by the NHTSA. Passengers usually experience less force in a school bus accident than in a car accident. The tall, padded seat backs on a school bus create a protective compartment for a child.

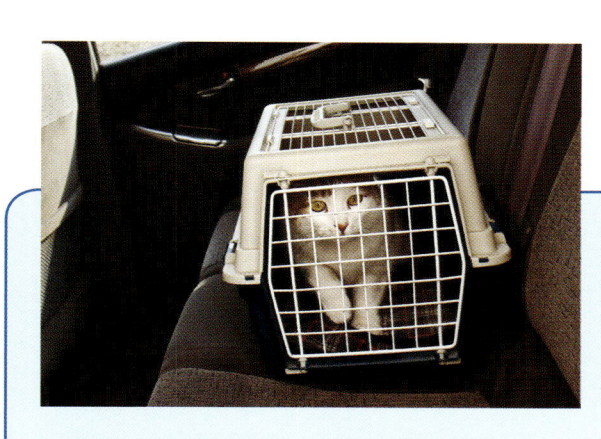

▲ There are different ways to keep pets safe in cars.

Keeping Pets Safe

Follow these steps from the American Society for the Prevention of Cruelty to Animals (ASPCA) to keep pets safe on a car trip.

1. Never leave pets alone in a car. Extreme heat or cold can be dangerous for them.

2. Do not let pets ride in the front seat. They are safer in the back seat.

3. Restrain pets so they don't get bounced. There are crates, barriers, and even dog seat belts that can be used.

What procedures are recommended for keeping pets safe in cars?

11

Car safety has come a long way in recent years. It continues to develop at a rapid pace.

Driving Into the Future of
CAR SAFETY

Since the early 2000s, developments in car safety have grown quickly. New technologies keep making cars safer. For example, in 2008, tire pressure monitoring systems were put into all new cars. These systems have **sensors** that alert a driver to tire pressure problems. Low tire pressure can cause a car to be unstable. High pressure can cause a tire to burst. Eliminating tire pressure problems helps drivers avoid accidents.

Lane departure warning (LDW) systems have become another key tool for driver safety. Sensors for these systems note where the lane lines are on the road. If a driver becomes distracted and drifts out of a lane, a warning is sent. This technology also sends an alert if another car is in the driver's blind spot, where the driver can't see it.

Another safety development is the driver status monitoring system. Like an LDW, this system uses sensors. The sensors, stored in the seat, monitor the driver's attention to the road. The system can sense if the driver's eyes are not on the road, or if the driver has fallen asleep. It can then send a beeping alert to the driver.

Adaptive cruise control is another new technology. It adjusts a car's speed to keep it a safe distance from the car in front of it. While this technology helps drivers moving forward, other new technologies deal with backing up. Rear parking sonar and a camera watching behind the car make for safer driving in reverse.

While seat belts and air bags are not new, these technologies are improving constantly. One concept that may soon be a reality is the "air seatbelt-bag." This prevents a person from moving, provides cushion from impact, and supports the head and neck.

▲ the air seatbelt-bag

13

DRIVING INTO THE FUTURE OF CAR SAFETY

Are Electric Cars a Safe Ride?

One development in car safety involves using a different type of fuel. Today most cars run on gas. An alternative is the electric car or electric vehicle (EV). This car runs on electric energy. The energy is stored in powerful batteries.

In March 2012, President Barack Obama announced the EV Everywhere Challenge. The challenge was to make EVs more affordable and convenient than gasoline cars by 2022.

Some safety experts believe EVs are safer than gasoline cars. Unlike gas-powered cars, EVs do not store **flammable** gasoline in a tank. This means there is less risk of an explosion if the car is in a crash. Also, there are no poisonous fumes to inhale at the gas pump.

History of the Electric Car

Many people think of the electric car as a new technology. But the electric car has actually been around for more than a hundred years. Here is a brief history of it.

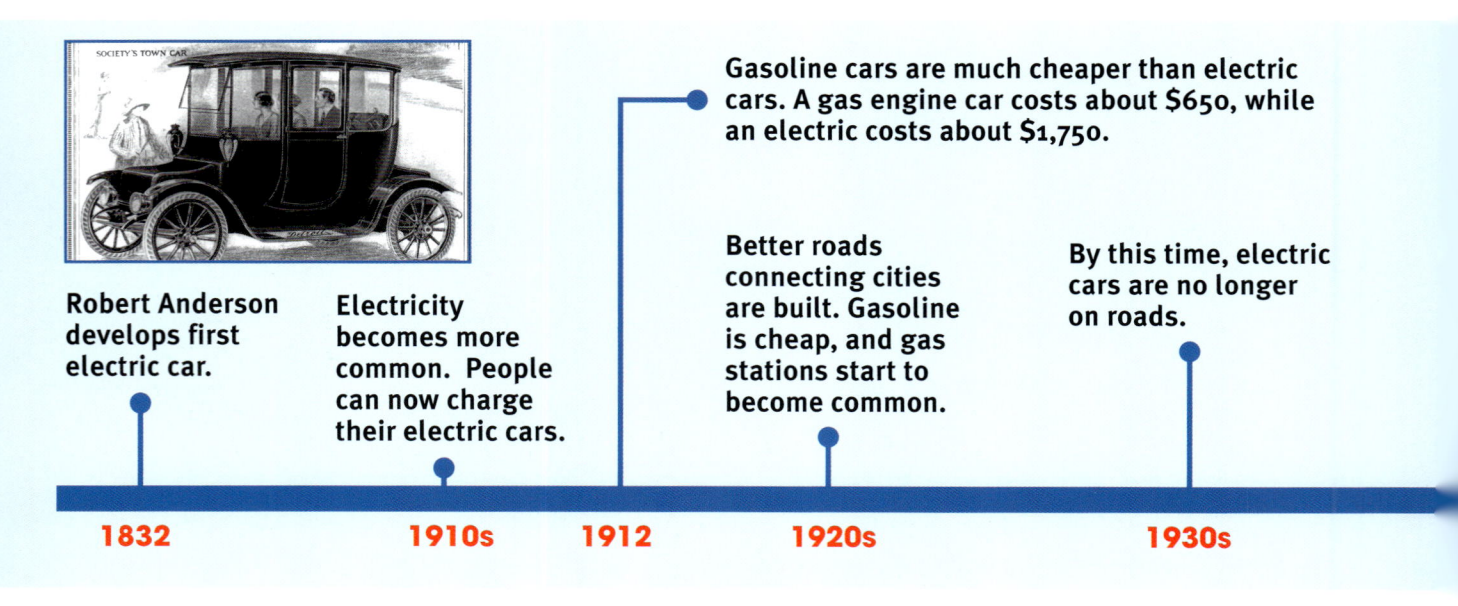

1832 — Robert Anderson develops first electric car.

1910s — Electricity becomes more common. People can now charge their electric cars.

1912 — Gasoline cars are much cheaper than electric cars. A gas engine car costs about $650, while an electric costs about $1,750.

1920s — Better roads connecting cities are built. Gasoline is cheap, and gas stations start to become common.

1930s — By this time, electric cars are no longer on roads.

14

It is also easier to control pollution from electric cars than from gas-powered cars. Therefore, EVs keep the air cleaner.

Finally, there is no engine in an EV. This means there are fewer moving parts and less chance of a breakdown that might lead to fire.

However, this doesn't mean that EVs are completely safe. According to *MIT Technology Review*, the safety risks of EV batteries are similar to the risks of storing energy for gas-powered cars. Any energy stored to move a car at fast speeds over long distances can cause problems.

The *Technology Review* notes that a high amount of energy stored inside the battery of an electric car can be a fire risk. However, safety regulations greatly reduce this risk.

Carmakers will likely continue to improve the safety features of electric vehicles. Jeff Dahn, a professor of physics and chemistry at Dalhousie University, says that even now, the risk of fire is tiny. According to Professor Dahn, if electric car batteries are used correctly, the risk of fire can be almost completely eliminated.

1976 — Congress passes a new law that supports research on electric vehicles.

1997 — The first hybrid electric vehicle goes on sale in Japan. Hybrids use two types of power, gas and electric.

2012 — President Obama launches the EV Everywhere Challenge. He wants to make electric vehicles as affordable as gas-powered cars by 2022.

2015 — Today there are about twenty-three electric and thirty-six hybrid model cars available. There are more than 230,000 electric cars and over 3.3 million hybrids on roads in the U.S.A.

Simulated Driving

Car safety experts are also focusing on teens. Teen drivers are more likely to be in car crashes than older drivers. So experts are rethinking the way that teens are taught to drive. They want to improve the safety of teen drivers.

That's where **simulated** or virtual driving comes in. Simulated driving may sound like a video game, but it's more than that. Simulators have pedals, steering wheels, and a wide screen to model the driving experience.

▲ Learning to drive on a simulator can help teens drive more safely.

Driving Age

In the 1920s, states passed the first laws on a minimum age for driving. By 1940, sixteen was the minimum driving age in most states. Since that time, there has been an ongoing debate about whether or how to raise the age.

PROS

People who want to raise the driving age point out that sixteen-year-old drivers have a higher crash record than drivers in any other age group. In states where the driving age is seventeen, the number of teen accidents is much lower.

CONS

People who want to keep the driving age at sixteen say that changing it would be inconvenient for some families. They claim that inexperience causes accidents, not age.

The state of Georgia has tested simulators. One hundred and fifty schools received simulators to use in driver's education classes. Since then, according to the Centers for Disease Control and Prevention, there have been many fewer teen fatalities.

Research at Wright State University in Dayton, Ohio, showed similar results. When teens used a simulator, their rate of car accidents went down.

Self-driving cars will communicate with, and be aware of, everything around them.

Cars Without Drivers

Most accidents are caused by driver error. Companies have been working on driverless cars for many years. These cars would eliminate driver error.

Driverless cars will have many benefits. They will lower the number of traffic accidents and help with traffic jams. However, what is actually possible right now is quite different from what people imagine.

"Autonomous driving is not going to mean jump in the car, push a button, say 'Take me to grandma's house' and go to sleep," says James Bell, head of consumer affairs at General Motors car company. "That may come someday, but not soon."

The first driverless cars will use sensors, which make the cars **semiautonomous**. First, some sensors will allow the car to detect signs and people on the road. Next, other sensors will ensure that the car knows where it is at all times. And most importantly, there will be sensors that tell the car what action to take in every situation.

The more advanced driverless cars become, the more they may be able to interact with other cars and with the road. For instance, stoplights could automatically turn green if there are no other cars around. **Autonomous**, or fully self-driving, cars may not be as far away as people think.

Are Self-Driving Cars Good or Bad?

PROS

Self-driving cars check everything around them. They regulate speed. They avoid human error. They will allow the young, elderly, handicapped, and those who cannot drive to get around easily.

CONS

Drivers are more likely to get distracted in driverless cars, even if they know they still need to pay attention. This makes them less able to react when necessary. Also, children won't be able to go in these cars alone since they can't drive if the auto-drive function gets turned off. And the cars might not work well in rural areas, where there are fewer computerized items for the car to read.

This self-driving car has a roof sensor to detect light and location.

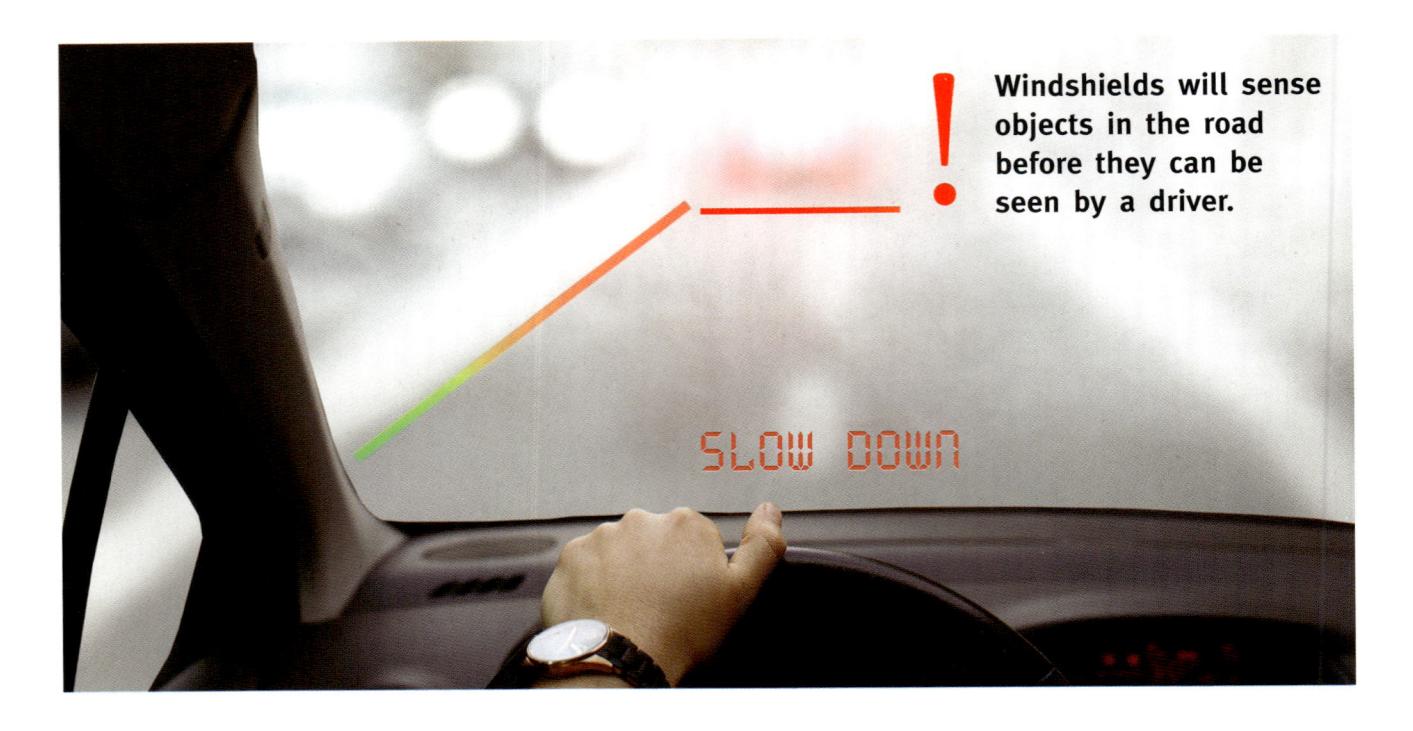

Windshields will sense objects in the road before they can be seen by a driver.

Will Cars Have Minds of Their Own?

Many of the latest car safety features being developed could make cars seem as if they have minds of their own. Here are some features that are being developed for future cars.

An **augmented** windshield will alert a driver to an object ahead on the road, like an animal. It will also give information about attractions as the driver passes by them. A future car will also automatically brake if an obstacle is sensed. And the headlights will adjust to create more light on the road.

The car will slow down when it senses that a traffic light around the corner has turned red, even though the driver cannot see it yet. It will also message the cars around it to slow down.

Slippery roads will no longer be a problem. The car will send more power to the wheel that has the most **traction**, or grip. Headrests and seats will be able to sense changes during an accident, preventing whiplash. If a rollover seems likely, the car will apply selective braking to try to prevent it.

Road Safety

Cars are not the only part of driving that is becoming safer. Roads are also changing. Here are some possible developments.

GLOW IN THE DARK ROADS
In the Netherlands, some roads are testing a paint that glows at night. It would charge through solar power during the day and then glow for eight hours at night.

ELECTRIC PRIORITY LANES
Electric cars are here, but there are not a lot of places to charge them. These roads would help with that. Magnetic fields built into the lane would charge the car as it drove.

SOLAR ROADWAYS
Solar panels in roadways would charge with sunlight during the day. Heat from the panels would help keep the roads ice-free in winter.

ANTI-ICE ROADS
These pavement surfaces contain natural substances that prevent ice from forming.

Where to Next?

The future of car safety technology is exciting. Predicted to come soon is a rear-facing infant car seat that installs itself. This car seat will install automatically when paired with a smartphone app and the car's safety system. The app will also monitor the car seat to make sure it's always in place.

One car company is thought to be working on special sensors. These sensors would follow the driver's heartbeat and other body systems. If the driver is in danger, this car would drive off the road and call 911.

Wherever the future takes cars, safety will always be the top concern.

▲ What safety features will future cars like this one need?

Predicting the Future

Isaac Asimov was a science professor and a science fiction writer. Asimov wrote and edited over 500 books. He wrote about the problem of human error in driving many years ago. He attended the 1964 World's Fair in New York. Afterward, he wrote an essay in the *New York Times*. He imagined what the world would be like fifty years in the future. Among his predictions were robot (or self-driving) cars. He wrote, "Much effort will be put into the designing of vehicles with 'robot brains'—vehicles that can be set for particular destinations and that will then proceed there without interference by the slow reflexes of a human driver." It seems Asimov's prediction will soon come true.

GLOSSARY

augmented (aug-MEN-ted) *adjective* made better and more useful (page 20)

autonomous (au-TAH-nuh-mus) *adjective* able to work without a controller (page 19)

collisions (kuh-LIH-zhunz) *noun* clashes that happen when two or more people or objects hit one another (page 8)

fire-retardant (FIRE-rih-TAR-dent) *adjective* made to resist burning (page 5)

flammable (FLA-muh-bul) *adjective* easily set on fire (page 14)

semiautonomous (seh-mee-au-TAH-nuh-mus) *adjective* able to do only some functions without a controller (page 19)

sensors (SEN-serz) *noun* devices that signal an activity based on changes they detect (page 12)

simulated (SIM-yuh-lay-ted) *adjective* a version that is not real but is made to mimic the real thing (page 16)

traction (TRAK-shun) *noun* a friction that helps hold an object on a surface, such as a road (page 20)

INDEX

air bags, 9, 13
Asimov, Isaac, 22
autonomous, 18–19

Dillon, Austin, 4–5
electric cars, 14–15, 21
seat belts, 7–11, 13

self-driving cars, 19, 22
sensor, 9, 12–13, 19, 22

ANSWER TEXT EVIDENCE QUESTIONS

Use text evidence from both texts to answer these questions.

1. Look at the time line on page 7. What important concept was introduced to cars in 1947? Why was this important?

2. According to the first sidebar on page 11, how does the concept of tall, padded seat backs promote safety?

3. Look back at information on pages 5 and 12. What specific information explains how new technologies address safety issues?

4. Look back at Are Electric Cars a Safe Ride? on pages 14–15. What specific information does the writer use to explain the benefits of an EV?

5. Simulated driving is discussed on pages 16–17. What specific information explains the concept that using a simulator makes teens safer drivers?

6. Look back at page 19. What information does the author use to explain the procedure for how sensors work in self-driving cars?

7. According to the information on page 20, what are some concepts being explored for future cars?

8. Using information from both texts, compare the development of safety features in cars from the first half of the twentieth century to recent years.